How To Blog for an Online Store

The Complete Step-by-Step Beginners Guide to Blogging for Your Ecommerce Business

Jonathan Eldridge and Robert Bustamante

Disclaimer

The following information is provided for information purposes only. Our opinion is given based on our experience and not to be considered legal or professional advice. Please consult with a qualified attorney, tax accountant, and other professionals to ensure you are proceeding correctly. Our information is provided as an opinion of our experience and we do not warrant, represent, or provide any guarantees as to the suitability or outcome you may have.

We reference and link to third party services. Some of these third party links are affiliate programs that we may be compensated for in the event you sign up. The use of these third party services does not guarantee any success and or earnings for your business. Furthermore, we do not guarantee any information, instruction, or opinion of these products or services. Readers are advised to do their own due diligence when deciding on a suitable company or fit for their business needs.

Readers of this book agree that Certatim, LLC, all officers and owners are not responsible for the success or failure of your business decisions related to any information provided in this book.

Thank You

I want to thank you for purchasing our book about Blogging. You have made the first step and that's acknowledging that blogging is a powerful traffic builder.

In this book I'm going to show you how we have effectively been driving people to our online businesses with blogs.

This traffic has been instrumental in building our businesses online. We will walk you through step by step so you can follow along.

We link to sites and posts throughout the book and I understand that many of you are reading hard copies.

I have organized all these links into a free download that you can get on our site. Additionally I'm including a couple of other free gifts.

You can get our list of over 50 online resources we have used to generate over $1,000,000 online. I'm also including some template agreements for freelancing.

To get this free gift you can go
to http://www.longlivetheinternet.com/blogging-book

Once again thank you.
From
Jon & Bob from Long Live The Internet
http://www.longlivetheinternet.com

Table of Contents

Chapter 1 - Blogging
Content is King
Free Traffic
Be Consistent
Building an Audience
Give Them What They Want
The Blended Mix
Long Road

Chapter 2 - Topics
Listicles
You Are the Best
How To
Interviews
Opinions and Tone

Chapter 3 - Keywords
What is a Keyword
Finding Keyword Phrases
Google Keyword Planner
Breaking Down The Results
Looking in the Ruff
Understanding Google
What is Organic Anyhow?
The Golden Free Tool
Can I Compete
My Secret Keyword Finding Tool

Chapter 4 - Doing the Dirty Work

Writing means writing

Relate With the Reader

Google Doesn't Have Eyes

Email Opt-ins

Call to Action

Outsource

Hemingway

Chapter 5 - Dressing It Up

I Like Some Blogs and Dislike Others

Graphic and Photo Sites

Graphic Outsourcing

Spacing and Font

Subheaders

Chapter 6 - SEO

Blog Titles

The Slug

Keywords in Your Copy

Your Images

Meta Description

Links in your Blog Posts

Chapter 7 - Sharing Your Post

Webmaster Tools and Analytics

Backlinks

Email Your People

Get Social

Reach out to Influencers

 Commenting on Blogs

RSS feeds

Chapter 8 - It's Your Turn

Free Gift

Blogging

Content is King

We are going to outline the steps taken to do this. You don't need lots of money and you shouldn't be intimidated. We will walk you through the different steps and outline the tools and pitfalls that have helped us build half a dozen successful online businesses. Avoid the mistakes we made and you can launch in half the time and for half the cost.

More and more people are starting online stores daily. It's becoming more difficult to find your customers. Making a name for yourself can cost you a ton of money if you try and do it by advertising.

But maybe that isn't the best route to take. Maybe you could earn your traffic the good old fashioned way. Maybe you could create great content and people would share it. Those people would then find your store and shop on your site.

While this sounds great, it's just not true. Writing great content isn't enough to get your site found. Blogging has become an art. Unfortunately the art is less about writing, and more about marketing.

What should you be writing about?

Who should you be targeting?

How will your blog post be found?

How do you share your blog posts?

If you are struggling with blogging or just thinking about getting started this book is for you. Blogging for your online store is an art and we are going to teach you.

In this book we're going to explain to you step by step how to write a blog. We are going to look at what to write about. We will discuss how to get found, and how to drive sales to your online store.

We will go through tried and true techniques that we are using now. These are techniques that we have used to drive over $1,000,000 of sales to our online businesses.

So sit back, put on your thinking cap and let's do this.

Free Traffic

So what's the big deal about blogging anyhow? I understand that content attracts traffic. Aren't there other ways for me to attract this traffic? I can get traffic from social networks and I can pay for ads all over the internet.

Why should I bother committing time to blogging and creating content?

Let me tell you why.

Blogging takes time and consistency but its work for long after you finish. Let me explain.

It takes times to write your blog post and make it look good. Whether you are outsourcing part of the process or doing it yourself, you still have to organize your blog.

Once it's published though, it's in the wild forever. You are going to spend time sending people to the post and sharing it. But let's assume for a second that you didn't.

Let's assume you published your blog post and left it for dead.

The good news is that it does not die. Once you publish your post and its indexed by Google, it's there forever. Assuming your post is not time sensitive like "2015 Hairstyles," you have evergreen content.

You blog post will exist in the search engines and act as tiny little webs on the internet. They will continue to show in search results and bring traffic to your site.

As you site ages and increases its authority, your posts will mature with it. This will continue to bring you traffic at no incremental cost.

I know I said Free Traffic but this isn't really true. Your time is money. You may decide to pay for a copywriter, web designer, graphic designer or any other service related to blogging.

The good news is that there are no extra costs. Your blog post will live forever and that means there is a decreasing cost of each additional visitor to your site.

This traffic builds and builds and while some posts may only get a couple of visits a week, others will be far more successful.

This increased traffic results in more brand awareness and traffic. These additional people convert to sales.

Be Consistent

Unfortunately blogging is not something that you can do once and cross off the list. Blogging is a commitment. It takes time and it takes consistency.

Too often you see sites with three or four blog posts dated from a couple of years ago. This is not going to work.

You need to be consistent and you need to be committed. If you don't hold yourself accountable than nobody will.

Having an online store is time consuming. When you are starting out, you are wearing many hats. You are the accountant, the buyer, the support rep, the marketer and now I'm asking you to blog.

I know. It's a lot.

I'm not saying it's easy. I'm saying that you have to put time in.

There are options. You don't have to blog.

But if you are trying to build a large business that generates substantial revenue, blogging is crucial. If you don't want to spend a fortune on advertising, you must blog.

Setting a realistic goal though is important. Blogging takes far more time than you think. Depending on your site and the topic, it can take up to a full day to write and publish a blog post.

You probably won't spend an entire day in one seating. You may write your rough draft in a couple of hours and then come back and clean it up later. Then you may make graphics on another day and publish on another day.

The time ads up. My wife currently blogs once a week on her fashion jewelry site. (LoveandPieces.com) I can tell you, it's far more time consuming than she realized. She currently has someone writing the post. She then has another person creating the graphics. With all that help it still takes time to put it all together.

This is not to discourage you but I want to be honest about the work involved. Her particular industry is an image conscious one. It's important for her posts to be quality and look beautiful as well. Not every stores blog requires this attention.

Regardless, you have to be consistent. Staying consistent keeps you focused. My wife sends out an email every week and in that email is a link to her newest blog post. This system keeps her organized and accountable. The email has to go out and it has to link to a new blog post.

My recommendation is to start blogging once a month. Set a firm date and commit to it. Maybe you start with publishing every first Tuesday of the month. If you are publishing on Tuesday then that means you should have the writing done before the end of the prior week.

If the writing is done by Friday then you have the weekend and Monday to make your blog post look good and add graphics.

You must have a schedule. If you keep your blogging schedule loose, it won't happen. It's like going to the gym. You skip one day and then another and then it's been three weeks since you have been.

Mark your calendar and publish on the same day. You can always increase your pace or scale it back if you need. Don't do it without making a conscious decision and adjusting your schedule. If you don't treat it seriously, it won't happen.

In the next section we will talk about the different types of blogging and how to make them work for you.

Building an Audience

There are two real approaches to blogging. Each of them are different in some ways. Let's take a look at the two variations and then discuss how we can make both of them work for your store.

The first approach to blogging is building a community. Let's call this first approach "Building an Audience."

This particular approach is one of the things that I wish I had done sooner in my online career. I have built many software solutions and sites over the years. Unfortunately, I never tied them all together with a community. Bob and I never built a name for ourselves behind our brands. At the time, I didn't see the value to creating a community.

I was wrong and communities are an extremely powerful asset. People make buying decisions for many reasons. One of the main reasons is that they are comfortable.

You have done it yourself. Think about when you are shopping for a car. When you arrive at the car lot, you already know you are interested in the car.

Suddenly a car salesman approaches you. A good salesman gets to know you. He asks questions and listens. He tells you what you want to hear and addresses your concerns.

A lousy salesman just speaks. He goes through the paces and ignores what you are saying.

At the end of the small talk, it comes down to a buying decision. If you are comfortable with the person and place, you are going to proceed. If you aren't, you probably are going to leave.

The only difference here between these two scenarios, was the salesman.

The irony is that the salesman will be gone the minute you drive off the lot. You can just buy from either salesman and it not really change anything about the car. Arguably they both are going to be able to get you the same type of deal.

But you don't feel comfortable. You aren't committed to buying. My friend Danny just told me this exact story. He had gone to the Jeep dealership and was completely turned off by the salesman. The guy wouldn't listen to him. He was ignoring him and acted like he was doing Danny a favor.

Dan left and went over to the Infiniti dealership. He told me that he wasn't even sure he liked the Infiniti or wanted to spend that much money. Long story short, the salesman was incredible.

He walked Danny through all the features and options and sold him the car. Danny drove off the lot that day with an Infiniti because the salesman made him feel comfortable.

This is our first type of blogging. Building a community where people feel comfortable. Bob and I have been doing this on our newest venture Long Live The Internet. Building a community is about being honest with people. Telling your story. Whatever your story may be.

With the proliferation of social networks and reality TV voyeurism is the new norm. People are fascinated with following other people's lives. For better or worse, it feels like an episode of Big Brother. Through Facebook and Instagram, you can follow people around and watch their every meal.

It seems ridiculous, yet millions of people are doing it every day. Fashion bloggers are making a living taking photos of their daily outfits. People can't get enough.

So who are we to not give people what they want. In order for people to be comfortable, they want to buy from people they know. They want to hear stories they can relate to. On Long Live The Internet, Bob and I share our online business stories. We talk about successes and failures. Sometimes they are entertaining and sometimes they aren't. Either way, we are transparent and people enjoy this. We would love you to follow along by the way.

This approach is an effective way to engage your audience. You can make people comfortable with you and your brand. You are trying to sell products online. As we discussed, comfort is a large part of their purchasing decision.

By writing and sharing your experiences, people can relate to you. If they can relate to you, they are more inclined to buy from you.

Sharing your experiences and writing about your life doesn't have to directly relate to your store. People are interested in a face behind a brand.

Either way, telling stores is a long road. You need to understand that this is a longer approach to blogging.

This approach is based on building a community and building a following. This is not an approach that is going to get search engine rankings for your specific product or offerings.

Let's take a look at an example. Bobs wife has an online store Baby Love Luna selling children's clothes. This summer they rented and RV and took it through various states staying at campgrounds along the way. They traveled with 3 children all under 5 years old.
Yes they are crazy and there is no chance I would do this.

This made for an incredible opportunity for her to document and write about here experience. While the blog posts aren't loaded with keywords, they are loaded with personality.

They show a true story of a family with small kids travelling. This is great content. This is content that people can get behind and enjoy.

It's a real life example where people can get comfortable with her. This comfort ultimately results in sales for her online store. The people that follow her were incredibly interested.

This is one of those experiences that a lot of people think about doing. Showing her children and the stories they have, builds content for her online store.

Building a community is the long way. It's a sincere way, and one that people love. It's longer lasting and more engaging. If you have the time and the commitment, 9 times out of 10, this is going to be a more effective route. Your conversion rates will be superior.

Give Them What They Want

Now that you understand "Building an Audience," Let's look at the second approach. We are going to call this approach "Give Them What They Want."

The majority of people using the internet start by going to Google. They type in what they are looking for and up come the results.

Having your site show up is a valuable opportunity that you can't afford to ignore. Unfortunately these results are controlled by Google. Google is the gatekeeper to the Internet.

So like it, or not, you need to understand how Google works and what they are looking for. We will go into detail about this process later in the book.

For now let's talk about our second approach to blogging. This is the less personal approach. The idea is to attract an audience to your store. You aren't looking for any old audience.

You want engaged people. You want people with like-minded interests. Let's look at an example. Let's assume that you have started an online store selling Tupperware. Not the Tupperware brand but your new amazing leak proof, food storage containers.

Within a couple of blog posts, you are going to find it difficult to continually discuss your containers. You are going to be blue in the face from explaining how the lids are tight and they don't leak.

But you still need content to write about. What you are trying to do is attract people who are interested. This is done by writing about other topics they may be interested in.

For example. I was on Pinterest yesterday setting up a Promoted Pin advertising campaign for my wife.

I came across a beautiful picture of a strawberry salsa. I know this sounds ridiculous but I was actually drawn to the picture. The title was "5 Ingredient Strawberry Salsa." I was intrigued. I don't even know what Strawberry salsa is but the picture looked good.

I didn't have time to click through but wanted to use this example. This is a perfect blog post for your container store. You can discuss how the salsa is made. After the recipe you can highlight how your container can be used for mixing and storing the salsa after serving it.

This a related post that doesn't directly talk about your storage containers. It does however, appeal to like-minded people. The people interested in that recipe, are potential customers of your storage containers.

This example about the recipe is loosely related to containers. There are other, more direct approaches, you can use. Let's stick with the Tupperware store for simplicity. Let's think about some closely related blogging ideas that are directly related.

Here are some examples of blog posts that could be used:

· What Is Freezer Burn?

· How to Keep Lettuce Fresh

· 5 Essential Tools for Any Kitchen

· How To Freeze Fruit

These are just four ideas of topics. These may seem like random topics but they are based on things that people are actually searching for.

The idea is to "Give Them What They Want." As we discussed earlier, people are searching millions of topics every second through Google.

They are looking for answers to questions that you can answer. Many of these questions are relevant to your offering. They are being asked by people who would buy your products.

So why not give them what they want?

This approach focuses on specific questions or keywords. You blog about what they want to know. We will look at how you find these phrases later.

Once you have decided on your topic, you will write a post for this topic. If you are writing about "How To Freeze Fruit," you are going to give it your all. You are going to show pictures and explain step by step. You may even include a YouTube video.

You will give pointers and tips. Show what to do and what not to do. This helps to make your page a valuable resource for this specific question. Your goal is to rank for this specific question in the search results.

The next time someone goes to Google and types in "How To Freeze Fruit," you want to show up in the results. This can be an extremely rewarding approach with quick results.

I have oversimplified this process quite a bit here. The idea now is to get an idea of the concept. We will dive into the details later on.

Why guess on blog topics or write in the dark?

You can produce content that people are actively looking for? Give them what they want.

The Blended Mix

The two different blogging styles are completely different. Let's look at some of the pros and cons of each.

- Build an Audience

    Pros
- Make your reader comfortable
- Show your real personality
- Remove some obstacles to the sale
- Create a long term customer

    Cons
- Writing can't be outsourced
- It takes a long time to build an audience
- Posts may not be directly related to your product
- It's tougher to build authority for your site around keywords

- Give Them What They Want

    Pros
- People are instantly looking for what you have written
- Quick to rank in search engines and bring traffic
- These people are interested in your specific offering
- You can easily weave your product offerings into the story
- Can be outsourced and written by others.
- Quickly build keyword relevance for your site

    Cons

- High bounce rates on traffic (People leave your site quickly)
- Less committed readers
- Strangers that you haven't built a relationship with
- Low conversion rates on sales

As you can see there are a lot of factors to consider with the two different blogging types. I like to recommend that people start with a mix. Consider incorporating a little of both in your blog.

There is no law that says you need to commit to one type of blog style for all your posts. The beauty of blogging is that you can combine both of these techniques.

Maybe one week you write personal posts and tie them into your offering. On another week you give them what they want and write keyword related posts.

I find this the most rewarding approach to blogging. A happy balance combines a story that people can relate to while answering a question that people have.

This is the approach that Bob and I us on our blog Long Live The Internet.

If you provide value , answer questions, and tell a story about yourself, you can get the benefits of both approaches. You can build your community while attracting search engine traffic.

Long Road

We have covered the different approaches to blogging. Now we are going to talk about the reality of blogging.

You may not want to hear what I'm going to tell you.

Blogging is not a quick fix. Blogging is a perfect example of the tortoise and the hare. Blogging takes time.

Millions of people decide to start blogs daily. The majority of them peter out after a month or two. The few that survive, understand the commitment to long term traffic building.

Starting out, you may feel like you are writing for nobody. I'm here to tell you to stick with it.

This is not going to attract thousands of views and website visitors instantly. This takes time. The same way that you knew that building your online store was going to take time, blogging takes time.

Blogging is one of many different avenues you will need to pursue to continue to drive traffic to your site. The good news is that it can be rewarding and it's the gift that keeps giving.

As you continue to build your sites authority, your site will continue to improve in the search results.

Posts that you wrote months ago will start to get more authority. This authority will slowly push these old posts higher in the search results.

You will start to build traffic where there was no traffic before. Some posts will be an instant success. These may rank organically in the search results right away. They may drive legitimate traffic to your online store.

Other posts will flop. You will spend hours writing and making the perfect blog post only for it to be read by your mother and friend.

It's OK. Stay the course. It's a long road.

We are going to discuss tactics to gaining exposure later on.

The point to take away here is that some things work and some things don't. This is not an exact science and you will need to be committed to trying new things and modifying your techniques.

Keep your eye on the prize and continue to generate relevant content.

[2]

Topics

One of the most common things I hear from people with an online store is that they don't know what to blog about.

"I have nothing to talk about"

This is absurd. There are endless topics you can write about. That statement is an excuse. It's easier to say I have nothing to write about than to actually write.

Quite frankly you could write about not having anything to write about.

To prove it, here is a paragraph for your entertainment.

Blogging can feel so daunting when you have nothing to share with anyone. Millions of people are looking online to learn and be enlightened. I find myself unable to provide any knowledge or any information about anything. Truthfully I have nothing to share. You see, I don't eat, or sleep. I have no existence. I'm a person that can't provide any insight into anything. This makes me useless. Or does it? What if I became the most famous blogger writing about nothing? What if I wrote paragraph after paragraph, day after day, about not being able to share anything with anyone? Would this be story? Would I then be telling a story? But that's something. So by writing about nothing I would actually be writing about something?

You get the point. You can write about anything. If you get dressed in the morning there is a story there.

I read an article the other day about how Obama has someone select his outfits the night before. He doesn't want to decide what he is wearing in the morning. He has enough decisions to make that he feels this is one he shouldn't waste a minute on.

I agree with that and find it fascinating. It's a blog post in itself. If you brain is thinking, you have ideas. But I understand that writing is harder. Some people struggle to actually write.

That's why I'm going to give you a breakdown of some effective techniques for creating blog topics.

Listicles

You may not have heard of the term Listicle, but you have seen them. Let me give you some examples.

The 50 Most American Americans in History, Ranked

The 21 Oldest Pizzerias in America

12 Grilled Pizza Recipes that are Perfect for Summer

40 Things You Have to Do in Vegas Before You Die

These are examples of Listicles. All these came from a popular site Thrillist. They do nothing but listicles.
A listicle is defined by wikipedia as:

An article on the Internet presented in the form of a numbered or bullet-pointed list.

Listicles are hot.

A recent BuzzFeed listicle called "21 Pictures That Will Restore Your Faith in Humanity" has attracted more than 13 million views. The word Listicle comes from a combination of a list and an article.

Listicles work. Many people are lazy and looking for instant gratification. Listicles appeal to these traits. You can quickly get the content and gist of an article by reading a quick list.

We are slowly being trained to want more in less time. A listicle does just that. Scroll down a list of 10 recipes your mother-in-law will love. If you see one that catches your eye, you can read further about it.

They are catchy, effective, and easy to write. There are endless listicles you can use for your online store.

Are you selling sports memorabilia? Try sports trivia listicles.

Are you selling horse racing hats? Write some listicles on famous hats. Best horse racing hats or best royal wedding hats.

The topics are endless and are easy to come up with. First come up with the list. Then write a few sentences about each item on your list. Sandwich it between an intro and closing paragraph and you're done.

My wife did one about the 10 Ugliest Thanksgiving Jewelry Pieces and it still drives traffic to this day. To get an idea of some listicles ideas take a look at BuzzFeed and ZergNet. They both are loaded with listicle ideas that you can use for inspiration.

You Are the Best

This next technique is one that has worked extremely well for us. The idea is quite simple. For this example, we are going to create a listicle like we just discussed. This one is going to have a little twist. We are going to write it about influencers in our industry.

Your first task is to decide what specific group of people you would like to get exposure from. We are talking about people that have influence over your potential customers.

For this example we are going to use my wife's store to show you how she was able to put this trick to work for her.

To make some noise and get on the map, my wife decided she wanted to reach jewelry bloggers. She decided she would create a listicle about the Top Jewelry Bloggers. (12 Jewelry Bloggers You Should Be Following)
She wanted to get more exposure online. The easiest way to do this was to get some attention from these influential people.

After she decided the target influencer group, she put together a list of the actual jewelry bloggers.

The next step was to write a little blurb about each of the bloggers. You want to really praise them here. Pick something nice about their site or social network accounts or whatever you are writing about and play it up.

Make sure to include what differentiates them from the others and why they are so great.

Once you are done writing, you want to make your blog post look professional. We will talk later about using graphics and design. For this type of list, I recommend that you find an actual picture each person.

People love to see themselves. A nice picture, their name, and nice comments about them. It's too good for them to ignore.

If you can't find their picture on their website or "About Us" page, use Google Image Search. Type in their full name and chances are you can find their picture.

Put together your blog and proofread it. Make sure it looks great and it's ready for the lights and publish it. You want to reach out to these influencers immediately to let them know you have featured them.

Time is of the essence and you want them to know.

Below is the simple email my wife sent.

Hi XXXXXX,

My name is Elissa, and I'm the owner here at Love & Pieces.

I just wanted to let you know that we have just featured you and your site in our newest post of 12 Jewelry Bloggers You Want to Follow. You can see out article here: http://www.loveandpieces.com/blogs/online-jewelry-boutique-blog/19036563-12-jewelry-bloggers-you-want-to-follow

You are creating amazing content and we wanted to recognize it here at Love & Pieces. If you think your audience would find it interesting, please feel free to share the post as well.

Have a great rest of the week.

It's short, sweet, and resulted in an incredible response. Almost all the featured people shared the post and many of them linked to the actual page from their blogs.

As a result she currently ranks #1 in Google results for a highly competitive keyword at the moment.

This approach works. It's an easy way to get noticed, build relevant content, drive traffic, and generate sales for your site.

The How To

People absolutely love How To's. People love learning and calling your post a "How-To" makes it feel approachable.

A "How To" is a slang term for a detailed post where you teach the reader how to do something. For example. "How To Make A Paper Weight From Old Macaroni?"

You want to know, don't you?

How To's are effective blog posts and people love them.

The topics and options for your post are endless. In fact, this entire book is devoted to you learning "How To" blog for an online store.

Here are some things to consider when deciding and writing a "How To" post.

1.   Numbering the steps makes it easier to read and follow along

2.   Pictures are crucial and the more you can include the more engaging it is.

3.   Make sure your "How To" is related to the general theme of your store. You are trying to attract people interested in your product.

4.   Combine a listicle type title to make it more engaging. "5 Steps To Making a Macaroni Paperweight"

5. Don't forget to weave your product and recommendation into the steps.

6. People like details. Don't ever feel like you are giving too detailed of instructions.

How To's don't get old and are a great way to write a simple blog post. If you aren't sure how to do something yourself, Google it and learn. Then test it out and write your own post about it.

The options are endless. I would venture to say that I can come up with multiple "How To" posts for any online store. Here are a list of topics that we have found to be successful.

- Recipes
- DIY crafts
- Saving Money
- Beginner Tips
- Travel
- Fashion Advice
- Parenting

Interviews

One of the easiest ways to create a blog post is by having someone else create it for you. I'm talking about interviewing people and creating a blog post from their responses.

Think about your audience and your customers. What appeals to them? What would they be interested in? If it's not directly about your product then relate it to your industry.

My wife interviews a different jewelry designer each month and makes a blog post from it. She asks them to share images of themselves and other things that readers would like. It adds credibility to her site and designers are more than happy to get the exposure.

If you are selling something that isn't so straight forward, get creative. Let's assume you are selling baseball cards online. You can email a baseball historian that you can find online. Try emailing someone on the staff at a professional or amateur team. Both of these would be great interviews.

You will be surprised at the positive response you will get from an interview request. People are flattered when you ask them for an interview. Don't second guess yourself. Ask and don't be shy.

What's the worst that someone could respond?

No Thank You?

Big Deal.

Move on.

Make sure in your first email to give a little information about your company. Next you want to make sure you tell them why you are interested in them and why your audience would be interested in them.

Lastly make it clear that you will email them the questions or you can setup a call if they prefer not to write.

Leave it open and watch the responses you will get. Interviews are great for many reasons. Let's look at how you can use them to your benefit.

Reason #1 - The content is written by the person you are interviewing. People love to talk about themselves. If you ask leading questions, they will give you their whole lifes story.

Reason #2 - You can use this blog post as the focus of an email blast to your subscribers. People like to learn about other people.

Reason #3 - It adds credibility to your site. The fact that people are interviewing with you, makes your site seem like a credible source.

Reason #4 - Most people you interview are more than happy to share your blog post on their social channels. They help you spread the word about your site.

Reason #5 - It takes limited time to get this type of post done. Include pictures that you can get from the person you interview. Format the questions and you are done.

Reason #6 - You will most likely rank for the person's name in search results. This is an easy way to drive traffic from search for a person related to your site.

I recommend that you incorporate the Interview blog as much as you can on your site. Its quick, simple, and a win-win for all parties.

Opinions and Tone

My next topic is actually one that I don't think you should write about.

When I was little my mother always told me to stay away from religion and politics in conversation. She said people are sensitive about these things. They aren't going to be persuaded to believe your beliefs by arguing with them.

In a nutshell, the pros never outweighed the cons and I will take that advice to the grave with me. She was right. I stay away from these topics and I think you should stay away from blogging about them.

The purpose of this book is to help you blog for your online store. This is not a blog about your life or your views. The goal here is to drive more sales for your store.

This is done by attracting as many people as possible and making them comfortable with your store. You don't want to offend anyone or upset anyone.

You want them to spend with you regardless of their beliefs. You don't have to agree with their government policy, you just want to sell them a macaroni paper weight.

Blog neutrally and present both sides of any discussion. Don't pick a side. Be objective and let people take from it what they want.

If you are too opinionated, you risk scaring off a potential sale.

Lastly, you want to write positively. People don't want to focus on the negative. Have a positive tone in your writing. You want people to be excited and to shop.

You don't want to blog about "The 12 Saddest Days This Year." That's not going to get people in the mood to shop. Be positive and spread joy.

3

Keywords

The absolute first step in writing any blog is deciding what you are going to write about. The next step is to determine the keyword phrase you are going to focus on. Let's first look at what these terms mean.

What is a Keyword?

A keyword is one or more words strung together that people search for online. For example let's assume someone is performing a search for Tiger Sharks. They may enter "What is a Tiger Shark" into Google. The "keyword" or "keyword phrase" here is "What is a Tiger Shark."

These are the specific terms that we are going to optimize our blog posts for. Before you set out to write any blog post, you will decide on a specific keyword phrase. Most keywords with only one word are too competitive to try and optimize for. This is why we will focus on phrases.

Generally speaking, the more words in your keyword phrase, the easier it will be to rank. Unfortunately, there is an inverse relationship to the number of searches. Far more people are searching for "Tiger Shark" than "What is a Tiger Shark." The problem is "Tiger Shark" will be far more difficult to rank for than "What is a Tiger Shark."

You are going to need to find the balance of where you realistically can rank and terms with large numbers of searches. We will get into this in detail later in this section.

What is a Long Tail Keyword Phrase?

Long Tail keywords are three and four keyword phrases. They are going to be your bread and butter and are highly focused searches.

These keyword phrases are far less competitive and provide a great opportunity for you to rank in the search results. They have less individual searches often but don't be fooled.

As you can see from the graph below over 70% of all searches are actually long tail searches.

The Search Demand Curve

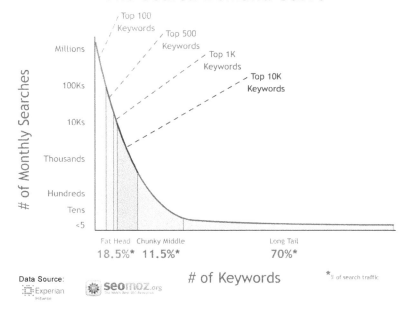

So we know that we need to pick a keyword phrase for every post. The next logical question is how to find keyword phrases.

How do we find keywords and which ones do we pick?

Finding Keyword Phrases

Let's start with the theme of your store. The first thing you want to do is start with a blank piece of paper. On that paper you are going to write down a list of all the terms that you believe are affiliated with your site. You can write things relate to your products or your industry.

For example let's look at a store that sells keychains online. Imagine the entire online store is devoted to keychains of varying types. Below is what that list may look like.

- **Key chains**
- **Keychains**
- **Key clasps**
- **Keyclasps**
- **Key hooks**
- **Keyhooks**
- **Keyrings**
- **Key rings**
- **Key finders**
- **Key cords**
- **Keycords**
- **Key locator**
- **Key light**
- **Key organizer**
- **Key clip**

You can see there are a ton of options. This list is what I can think of at this moment.

I don't have any knowledge of keychains but this is what came to mind. I'm sure there are many more. If you were a keychain retailer, I'm sure you could create a larger list.

You will note that I included some similar looking variations. I believe people may use two words instead of one when searching sometimes. For example "Key chains" is on the list and so is "Keychains."

This is far less of a concern nowadays. Google has started to recognize people's intent when searching. Regardless of whether people put the space between search terms, Google knows what they are looking for.

Google actually will show the same results in most cases for searches they deem have the same searching intent.

The reason I have it on the list though, is because we are going to use this to hunt for keyword phrases. While Google knows better, we don't want to rule out anything. There may be a keyword phrase using it one way or the other.

The next step in our keyword hunt is to summarize your current customer. Who do you believe your current customer is? Below is a list of who I believe would buy keychains online.

· Someone who is an avid collector of keychains (all ages)

·   Someone buying a gift for an avid collector of keychains (all ages)

·   Someone buying a gag gift for another person's special occasion (over 40, anniversary, birthday)

·   Someone looking for a specific niche keychain to address a problem they are having (floating for boaters, etc.)

Now you have your list of seed words and your potential buyers. The next step is to start to think about the pain points or interests that each of these type of people may have.

Let's take the last potential buyer on my list and dissect it a little further. Let's assume this is a boater who is looking for keychains. I assume he would want a keychain that floats for when he is on the boat.

This is a common concern and I can think of a ton of blog posts that would work to entice this person.

- 10 must have items to have on the boat

- Does your floating keychain actually float?

- Can you Name 5 things that should float on a boat?

- 4 Different Types of Keychains that float

- 3 Terrible tales of boaters who didn't have floating keychains

Now we have some interesting blog posts. These are just some that I was able to come up with now. If you put in some time, I'm sure you could think of a lot more.

But in this step we are just coming up with rough ideas. The key here is that we haven't isolated the specific keyword phrase. You will note with most of the titles, we could interchange the keyword phrase freely.

Let's take the title "4 Different Types of Keychains that float." Below are variations of the same title using the keywords from our original list.

"4 Different Types of **Key Organizers That Float**"

"4 Different Types of **Floating Key Clips**"

"Did You Know There Are 4 different Types of **Keychains That Float**"

"More Than 4 Variations of Floating Keyhooks"

"Whats The Difference In These 4 **Floating Key Rings**?"

You can see that all these titles are essentially the same thing. The difference is that we used completely different keyword phrases in each title. I have bolded the keyword phrase in the titles above.

These phrases though are based solely on our list though. We need a better way to know what people are actually searching for.

We don't want to guess what people are searching. That's why we are going to narrow down the keyword phrases strategically.

There are many ways to do this, but they all work on the same foundation. Search volume.

I will lay down the principles of this technique using a free tool from Google.

Once I lay down the basic principles of how this process works, I will tell you about the software that I use. This software reduces the time substantially. Unfortunately it's not free but we will get to that later.

Google Keyword Planner

Google generates over half of its revenue from paid search placements. These are the sponsored results that you see in search results on their site.

You can pay to have your site show up in the search results. Google has extremely powerful bidding tool. You bid against other advertisers to show up in search results for keywords of your choice.

Because Google wants you to bid for these placements, they have provided a free tool called keyword planner.

The keyword planner is an incredibly powerful tool that allows you to see detailed search data from Google. We are going to use this tool to focus in on a keyword phrase.

Your first step is to head over to Google Adwords and signup for an account. It's free to search and we are not advertising now. If you are already using AdWords to advertise, you can use the same account.
Once you have signed up, you can ignore all the prompts to start a campaign. We are not actually going to run through the process of creating search ads. We are going to use the free keyword planner tool.

At the time of this writing, you can find the keyword planner under the tools menu from the top of the screen. They tend to change this quite often.

You now are going to select to search for new keywords using a phrase, website, or category. You have the ability to enter some different things. This is where it gets fun. Don't get overwhelmed by the options. Stick with me here.

There are three different ways that you are able to search for keywords or keyword phrases with this tool.

1st Way - Keyword: This is what I use every time. This allows you to enter a word or keyword phrase and get ideas based on that word. For example if I entered "keychain float" this would then return all the related search terms to this specific phrase.

You can get as broad or specific as you want with this field. If you entered just "keychains" it would show you all the terms that people search for related to keychains.

2nd Way - Your landing Page: This approach lets you type in your website or webpage (a specific page on your site). Google then goes and reviews that page. It looks at all the text on the page and then gives you recommendations for keywords or keyword phrases related to that page. This is useful for advertising but not much for blogging.

Let me explain. If you are following my directions, you don't have a blog post yet because you haven't written it. We haven't written it because we haven't decided on a keyword phrase.

But we need a url to search with. Why not just use your homepage? This is a terrible idea. Your homepage probably has the least amount of text of any of your pages. The text is where Google is getting their keyword ideas.

For online stores, most of what is on the homepage are images. Google can't tell what the images are. They merely look at the text you have, the alt tags, and the image names.

We want keyword phrases we haven't thought of yet. We want new traffic. You can't really use this approach for blogging.

3rd Way - Your Product Category: Remember that this tool is designed for you to use with Googles advertising platform. They would love for you to pay to have your site listed for every search term in the world.

The category option lets you drill down to your category to find recommendations for keywords. I find the category tool vague and unfocused.

For example I have no idea what category keychains would fall into. The point of this exercise is to find highly focused keywords. This just doesn't work for that.

So we settle on the 1st way. You want to pay attention to the extra search options. You can search for specific languages, time frames, geographic location, and types of matches.

This is amazing if you think about it. Google is letting you see detailed information about their search results. This is your way to peak on the other side of the curtain for free.

Breaking Down The Results

So now I'm going to enter "keychain float" as my search keyword. I'm using the **1st Way** and then click on the "Get Ideas" button. You will be taken to another page which is actually the full Keyword Planner tool.

This is where you will spend most of your time and refine your results. The first thing you want to do when the page loads is to switch to the "Keyword Ideas" tab. When the page originally loads it shows the "Ad group ideas" tab. What this means is that Google clusters a bunch of related keywords together.

In my opinion they are pushing you to advertise for the whole group of keywords. I would like to see each individual keyword phrase. I like the granularity of seeing each keyword by itself.

> **NOTE:** I use the terms Keyword and Keyword Phrase interchangeably. Technically a keyword is one word, whereas a phrase consists of many keywords. Rest assured, I'm looking for the same thing. In reality, I almost never select a Keyword for a blog post. One word is almost impossible to rank for in the search results.

So now that we have selected the "Keyword Ideas" tab in the middle of the page you should see your specific search term at the top of the list. In my case I see "keychain float." Now comes the genius part of this tool.

Search Volume

If you look to the right you will see a column titled "Avg. monthly searches." This is actually the number of times people search for your exact keyword phrase. In my case it shows that 90 people search for the specific phrase "keychain float," each month, on Google.

The obvious question is how many searches are you looking for? Clearly the more searches, the better. The problem is, ranking for these popular search terms is more difficult. Smaller search volume usually has less competition. I like to focus on anything over 500 searches a month with about 2000 being a nice sweet spot.

Depending on your industry and the number of people selling similar items to you, it can be tough. The magic comes in finding the hidden terms.

Adwords Search Competition

The next thing you want to look at is the column to the right of searches titled competition. It's important to note that this is not competition for you. This is not how difficult it's going to be to show in search. This is the competition in AdWords. This is how many people are paying for these specific keywords.

This gives you an idea of the field and what you are up against. It's important to note competition in advertising is different than search. Just because someone is paying for results, doesn't mean they are competing in search.

We will look at that further in a minute. At this point you just want to see what you are up against. You can go one step further and look at the next column over.

This column is the "Suggested bid." Again this is not relevant for your organic search competition. It shows you what people are currently willing to pay for their ad on Google.

In my case for "keychain float" they are suggesting a bid of $0.82 per click. This probably means that someone is willing to pay $0.75 per click currently. Google does a nice job of creating a bidding war.

The importance here is to show that there is interest. If people are willing to pay for the click, then it must be valuable to them. There is clearly buying intent for this keyword phrase. We don't need to see buying intent on all our keywords.

It really depends on your particular search term and your intent with your blog post. Maybe you are just trying to build awareness for your brand with a particular blog post.

In that case your primary concern may be impressions only. You may just want the most eyeballs to be able to read your post. Regardless of whether they intend to buy, you want your post read and shared.

This is the case with my wife's blog post on popular jewelry bloggers. Her post about these bloggers was merely to get awareness about her brand.

There is no intent to buy when people are searching for this keyword. The competition is low. This is because someone is looking for a jewelry blogger and not actual jewelry. So naturally, there is less competition on AdWords.

Looking in the Ruff

Now that you know what you are looking at in the results, let's actually dig in.

My term "keychain float" actually came up and showed 90 average monthly searches. But I'm looking for the best term. There are dozens of variations of the phrase that all describe the same thing.

My first step when looking at other results is to click on the header "Avg. monthly searches." This sorts the search results by the number of searches each month. I want to see what is at the top and then work my way down.

Once you do this, you will see that the top of the list is actually filled with generic results. These are often terms that are unattainable and you should stay away from. In my case I'm seeing key chain, and key rings, and key holder.

"Key holder" is an interesting one. I didn't have that on my initial list when I started. This is one of the most searched terms, and I hadn't even thought about it. Add it to your list.

The beauty here is that you are able to see what people are searching for. This opens your eyes to terms you may not have thought of. But let's carry on.

These are all generic terms and unattainable now. I'm looking specifically for keychain floats or something related to it.

I keep scrolling down the list and realize that there are too many generic results. We will now click on the column "Keyword (by relevance)." This now re-sorts the results by relevance to my initial keyword "keychain float."

Now that I have done this, I look down the list and see my winner. "Floating keychain" has 880 searches. The competition is high but this is directly what I'm looking for.

Ad group ideas	Keyword ideas							Download	Add all (675)

Search terms		Avg. monthly searches	Competition	Suggested bid	Ad impr. share	Add to plan
keychain float		90	High	$0.82	–	

Show rows: 30 ▼ 1 - 1 of 1 keywords |< < > >|

▼ Keyword (by relevance)		Avg. monthly searches	Competition	Suggested bid	Ad impr. share	Add to plan
key chain		18,100	High	$1.56	–	
key rings		12,100	High	$1.63	–	
floating keychain		880	High	$0.80	–	
keychains for men		1,300	High	$0.92	–	

My initial keyword phrase would have been a huge mistake. With only 90 searches, this new keyword phrase has almost 10 times the search volume.

I have my keyword phrase now for my blog post. Next I want to see what my competition looks like in the search results.

Understanding Google

One of the keys to having your blog read and found is ranking in the search results. We are going to discuss later how we can increase our chances. For now it's important to first understand Google search results.

Let's take a look at a typical search results page for the terms "floating keychain."

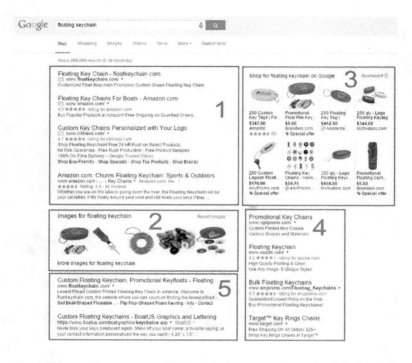

In the image above you will see 5 different sections that I have divided. Let's break down each section so you know what you are looking at.

1. This section is Google AdWords results. These are the sites paying per click for the specific search term "floating keychains." Google told you the competition was high and they weren't joking. There are a lot of people willing to pay for that search term.

2. Section 2 is actually one of the most under-looked sections of Google search results. This section is free and we are going to talk about how you can get your images to show in this section. It's amazing how few people are focusing on this trick.

3. This section is referred to as Google Shopping. This is also powered from Google AdWords but is actually a product feed. You can submit your products to Google to show in this section. You also pay per click the same that you would for page advertising. This is actually an incredibly high converting section. I highly recommend you consider setting up a Google shopping feed if you aren't already.

4. This section is also AdWords results. These people are willing to pay per click but maybe not as much as the ones from section 1. Determining whether you show in section 1 or 4 is determined by your sites relevance, stickiness, and your bid. That's for another book though.

5. Lastly section 5 is what we are targeting. This is the organic section. This image is a little misleading as the page scrolls down and there are 8 other results in section 5. Regardless, you can see how Google is making their money. What once was a simple search engine, is now a minefield of undercover ads.

What is Organic Anyhow?

I have used the term organic but maybe it's not clear what I'm talking about. I'm not exactly referring to vegetables. Organic search results are sites showing up in the results naturally. This means that they are not paid placements. These are sites that Google has deemed relevant to your search and has shown them on their own accord.

Ranking high in the search results can be incredibly profitable for your online store. The whole idea of blogging is to drive more people to your store and sell more goods. The irony of this term "organic" is that there is nothing organic about it.

Because it's so valuable to rank in the search results, people optimize or modify their content to do so. I liken this concept to the new buzzword GMOs. Everyone's blogs these days are using GMOs or genetically modified organisms to show higher in the results. We will get into some of those techniques later in the book.

Unfortunately using these GMOs is necessary to rank. While some people may tell you, "just create good content." It's not true. Good content by itself doesn't rank.

Often good content does get shared or linked to. It's these factors that actually result in the higher rankings. Don't believe me? Look at the first organic result in the prior image. Their domain name is www.floatkeychain.com. Coincidence?
No.

Strategic.

The Golden Free Tool

Now we have our keyword phrase and we understand what organic search results are. It's time to dive into the competition. This is the most important part of qualifying your keyword.

If you chose a keyword to blog about that is too competitive, you will never be found. It's a waste of your time. To see whether we have a chance, we are going to use another free tool.

Your first step is to go to Moz.com. Moz is a company specializing in providing software and education about search engine optimization. Their blog is one of the best in the business and I highly recommend the read. You can find their blog here at https://moz.com/blog.

To attract your business, Moz offers an incredible browser plugin tool for free. It works on Google Chrome and Firefox. You can download it here. Download Here.

> **NOTE:** If you aren't using Google Chrome as your internet browser, I'm sorry. You are using an inferior internet experience. You are doing it wrong. Chrome is faster and better and free. Period. Make the switch.

Background Information for Your MozBar

Before we dive into using the MozBar, we need to go over two crucial terms that you will learn to live by. Moz has created two variables that are the core to their search engine analysis. The first of their two variables is **DA** or Domain Authority.

Domain Authority: The measure of power or strength that a particular domain name carries in the search engine world. It's one of many factors considered in search engine results. It's a number on a 100 point scale. It's an indicator of how well a domain is likely to rank in Googles search results. DA is based on dozens of factors but generally Age, Popularity, and Trust.

For example google.com has a DA of 100 whereas floatkeychain.com has a DA of 12.
The next term to familiarize yourself with is **PA** or Page Authority.

Page Authority: This is defined as a measure of power of a particular page within your website. It's also a number on a 100 point scale. Page Authority is how likely a specific page within a site is likely to rank. The PA and DA are loosely affiliated with one another.

It is possible to have a higher PA on certain pages of your site than your DA and vice versa. This is because each page stands as a unique page in search results. Sites don't rank, pages do.

For example google.com has a PA of 79
whereas google.com/adwords/ has a PA of 91.

Back To The Bar

Not that bar. Get your mind back on track. I know that last part can be boring, but it's important. These terms are important for search engine rankings. You will need to consider these values for lots of things including outreach for your blog.

If you haven't already checked the DA of your own site, now is the time. You want to see what you are working with. Your **DA** is your juice. It's how powerful your site is and crucial to competing in the search results.

Below is a rough break down of **DA**

1-10: Just getting started and you really need to build up your domain authority. We can talk more about how that's done later but this is where many of you will be.

11-20: This is respectable. You can compete and rank for keyword phrases in the search results.

21-40: Solid. You are not unstoppable but you can start clipping the heels of some pretty big name sites with a **DA** in this range.

41-60: Your site is the real deal. You already have authority and all the needed pieces to blog and be successful with almost all your posts. If your page ranks here, you probably know most of what I've been sharing.

61-80: You are already a large company with ample sales. Save some for the little guys.

81+: Please close this book. You are wasting your time.

Can I Compete

We talked about finding your keyword phrase and we have established how to find your **DA**. The last part of the puzzle is assessing whether you can compete.

Is it even worth writing your blog post?

Your first step, for this part, is to go to Google and type in your keyword phrase. Make sure that your MozBar is on. You can click the little M in the top of the browser window to toggle it on and off.

If it's on, you will see little bars underneath each of the search results on Google. In each of these bars you will see the DA and PA for each result. Below is a picture of one of the results and what it looks like on my screen.

You will see in this search for "floating keychain" that this particular page has a DA of 12 and a PA of 17. This happens to be the number one organic result on Google.

So let's break this down a little. The first question is whether your DA is larger than this site. If you have a DA larger than this site, you are off to a good start. The next thing to look at is the PA. The

PA here is larger than the DA so this page is deemed relevant for this search term.

NOTE: In most cases highest PA wins in search results. PA is built on DA and other factors.

Although paid results don't affect our competition, let's look at them for informational purposes. Looking at the sponsored search results one of them appears to be Amazon. Amazon has a DA of 97 because they are behemoths but their PA is 1.

That means that the page is not valued strongly in search results. It would be difficult to impossible for Amazon to show organically for this specific keyword. They are competing against pages with higher PAs. They are paying so that puts them in the top but organically they don't show.

Back to the organic results, it's important to look at all results on the first page. You want to get a feel for what the competition is. Can you compete with these sites? If they have high DAs are their PAs very high as well?

For our example "floating keychain" our results look attainable. I believe that I could rank on this page. There are some pages with high PAs but the other results that have much higher DA rankings have PAs of 1.

Note these may be new pages that haven't received their appropriate PA number yet. When you first publish a page, Moz may take up to two months to give your page a PA. More likely they are tiny pages on huge sites like eBay and Bass Pro Shops.

These pages haven't been given high PAs and likely offer shallow content. Best of all, is the first ranking in the results. They have a DA of 12 which you should be able to compete with and a page authority of 17.

> **NOTE:** Don't be fooled by DA only. Many blogs actually host their sites at WordPress.com or Blogspot.com. While the domain has lots of authority, that's not what you want to look at in this case. You are more interested in the PA for sites that reside on domains like that. There are tons of meaningless pages on large DA sites. (PA of 1 or 0 even) You have to look at both.

Domains and Titles

I don't want you to get the idea that it's all about DA and PA. This is the most important measure, but there are other things you want to consider.

The domain name of the site that ranks number 1 organically is helping them a lot. Their domain name happens to be almost and exact match for our keyword phrase. This gives this site some extra hidden juice that isn't clear from looking at the DA and PA.

Google values that quite a bit. The reason they value this makes sense. If your domain name is almost an exact match for the keyword, chances are that the site is relevant for the search term.

It doesn't mean they are unbeatable. It just means you are going to have to offer that much better content. You will need to counter the extra juice received from the matching domain.

The other thing you want to look at are the Titles of the results. Do the titles have the exact keyword phrase in them?

For my "floating keychain" search, there are a couple that don't. For example one is "Collegiate Floating Fender Key Chain."

The more titles that don't have the exact phrase in the exact order, the easier it will be for you to rank.

Blog or Not To Blog

Based on these factors, I am comfortable blogging with the keyword phrase "floating keychain." There are low PA sites ranking. There are also sites without an exact match in the Titles. Lastly there are 880 searches a month for this term.

This is worthwhile blogging for. What's going to be my fictitious title for the blog I'm not going to actually write?

5 Floating Keychain Horror Stories

> **WARNING:** Once you have decided on a keyword phrase for your blog post, that's the only time you should use that exact keyword phrase for a post. Creating multiple blog posts with the same keyword phrase actually confuses Google.

The whole point of this exercise is to make each blog post optimized for a specific keyword phrase. If you have more than one post for the same phrase, how would Google know which one is the best result.

You are better off creating a new post with a similar keyword phrase. From your new post link back to the original post with it's original keyword phrase.

We will discuss this in more detail later in the book when we talk about linking.

My Secret Keyword Finding Tool

I understand that the process seems complicated. It can take some time to understand. I would recommend that you go back later and read the prior section a second time. This really is the core of how your blogs are going to be able to compete.

Once you are comfortable with the techniques, I want to tell you about my secret time saving tool. This process builds on all the knowledge you have from the last sections. As I mentioned before, this can save a ton of time. The bad news is that its not free.

This is the method that I currently use. The software costs $97. The good news is that I'm friendly with Spencer, who created Longtail Pro. He has agreed to give our readers a discounted price of $67. If you go to http://www.longlivetheinternet.com/longtail you can get our special discounted rate. Please don't share this publicly.
If you just want to try it out, there is a 10 day free trial. Let's assume you have downloaded the software and installed it. You will be prompted to enter your Adwords credentials during setup.

This is because LongTail Pro actually uses the same Keyword Planner Tool from Google. The beauty of this tool is that it combines the DA and PA from Moz with the search terms from Googles Keyword Planner.

You can refine your search based on various criteria. You can limit your keyword searches to only show keyword phrases that have over 500 searches a month. You can filter results to only show keyword phrases with more than 2 words and less than 3.

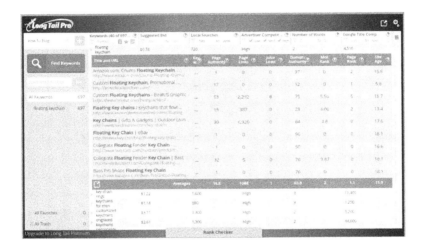

Quite frankly this software makes it much easier. I'm able to sort through and find potential keyword phrases much quicker. I don't want to come across as too salesy so I will leave it at that. Suffice it to say that once you have gotten the hang of what you are looking for, this makes it much quicker.

4

Doing the Dirty Work

Exhausted yet? All that work just to isolate the keyword phrase and make sure you can compete. I know it feels like a lot of work up front. This can save you lots of lost time though. Would you prefer to write you blog post only to find that it will never be found?

Take the guessing out of the process and do the leg work up front. With your isolated keyword phrase ready to go, it's time to actually blog.

Writing means writing

Unfortunately by definition, blogging means you have to blog.

Blog: An informational site or discussion, published online, consisting of individual posts in reverse chronological order.

From here, blogs have matured and there are millions of variations to the original concept. It doesn't really matter the exact approach you decide to take. Each post you write, regardless of how you structure your site is going to rank by itself.

The goal is to get customers to your online store. The point of this whole exercise is to widen your net and increase your sales.

We have shown that Google controls the traffic and google likes words. That means you need to write a lot and write smart. Writing smart can mean many things. We are going to look at what it means in the context of blogging for your store.

Google favors longer length blog posts. According to a serpIQ study, the highest ranking blog posts were over 2400 words.

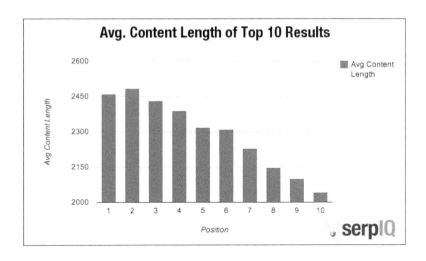

I know this seems like a lot of writing. There is something to note here. This is not the case for all keywords. This is probably true for the more competitive keywords but you don't have to write a love story for each blog.

The rule of thumb I use is no less than 500 words. I really don't want to ever publish a blog post less than this length. I have been able to get 500 word posts rank for highly competitive pages.

I have heard some say that 300 is the least you can have. I have not had effective results under 500 words. Google deems the content thin. The point here is to understand that length can help. People do enjoy long form writing and Google does as well.

Length though is one of many factors that is going to help your blogging.

Relate With the Reader

The next thing we are going to look at is drawing in your reader. I discussed earlier in the book how you can write using a blended mix of relating to the reader and giving them what they want.

Other factors that Google considers when ranking your site are bounce rate and time-on-site.

Bounce Rate: The percentage of people who visit one page on your site and then navigate away to another site after only viewing the one page.

Time on Site: The amount of time that a website users spends on your page before leaving to another destination.

Without getting too complex here, Google believes that longer visits, and multi-page visits, are better. If someone comes to your page and reads your post for 30 seconds and then clicks on the back button, this looks bad.

On the flip side if someone gets to your post and reads for 5 minutes and then clicks through to another page on your website, this is great.

Google uses these metrics to help measure engagement and people's enjoyment of the content. These among hundreds of other factors are used in your blog rankings.

So why am I talking about this? I'm saying this because people have short attention spans. When the average internet browser lands on your page, you have limited time to suck them in.

One of the most effective ways to do this is to tell them a story. People like stories even if they are silly. This is the easiest way to get them into the post and to continue to read.

While stories draw the reader in, it's important to not go too far. A good blended mix walks the line. If your post title was "5 Floating Keychain Horror Stories," maybe you start with your own story. A brief story that draws the reader in and lets them relate to you.

Without getting too detailed, you then lead into the actual meat of the post. This does a couple of things. First, the reader feels an instant connection with the writer. It's no longer an impersonal site and an impersonal post. They realize you are a real person.

Secondly we have kept the visitors interest and kept them on your site longer. We want them to get into the story and stay for a while. Maybe even buy something.

Google Doesn't Have Eyes

Many people mistake the phrase blogging for posting images. I suppose you could call this blogging but it's almost useless in the eyes of Google. Google doesn't have eyes. Google can read but it has no eyes.

When you post a bunch of images, Google can't see what's on those images. They can see and recognizes colors and shapes. Unfortunately they can't relate that to search and keyword relevance.

On the flip side, they are able to see ALT tags and file names. They use these clues to "see" an image.

They don't know that your images are pictures of hundreds of different floating key chains. You have to tell them using words. Explaining, and writing about them, allows Google to understand the context and content of the images.

We will discuss how you can use those tags and image names to your benefit later. The point here is to understand that creating a blog post of images has limited value. Google has to determine relevance and depth of content. Unfortunately they rely primarily on words to do that.

If you are posting images, they should be accompanied by substantial amounts of text. You will see this on successful bloggers who post videos or video interviews.

Almost all will write out a transcription of the interview or video and post it on the same page. Why do you think they are doing this? While it's helpful for people who rather read than watch a video, the primary reason is for Google. Google is then able to read what that page is about and can rank the page accordingly.

I don't want you feel like images are useless. That's not the point here. In fact we will discuss later how important images are to blogging. The point I want you to take away is that images on their own, are useless as a blog post. You must write and provide value through text.

Email Opt-ins

We have talked about engaging your readers and keep them on your page. Unfortunately the majority won't. Most people will leave your site after viewing one blog post. Many people will actually leave within seconds of landing on your page. This is reality.

Our job is to keep them as long as we can. Ideally they would actually buy something on their first visit to our site. The majority of the time though, they won't. It takes some people some time to warm up. For this reason, we want to do whatever we can to capture their email address before they leave.

Email has proven to be one of the most effective sales channels time and time again. In every blog post, I recommend that you have multiple spots asking people to join your email list. If you can capture the email address of your reader, you are far more likely to sell them something at a later time.

Add an opt-in to the side of your blog template. Put an opt-in in the middle of every blog post or at the end. You have to ask for peoples emails to get them. I wrote a detailed blog post on how my wife implemented this on her site successfully. I show you the free secret tool I used to double my wife's email opt-ins throughout her site.

If you don't currently have an email service, I would recommend using Constant Contact or MailChimp. Both of them are amazing and offer easy ways to create these opt-in boxes for your blog. You don't have to know how to code. They simply give you the code to paste onto the page.

Call to Action

Your post is now written and you have done your best to engage your reader. You did a great job of telling a story and you actually got them to read all the way to the bottom. Now what? Do you just leave them high and dry?

Absolutely not. This is your big chance.

You have earned their time and earned their interest. Now is the time to ask for the sale. At the least you want them to look around for a while. Here is what I would write at the end of my hypothetical blog post.

5 Floating Keychain Horror Stories closing paragraph would read something like this.

"Don't be the next horror story we write about. Take a look now at our amazing collection of affordable floating keychains. And as an added gift, enter the promo code: horror at checkout for 10% off now."

The idea is to lead them to the sale. This is what you wanted them to do in the first place. You put in all the time. You got them to read to the end. Don't leave them wondering where to go. Tell them what to do.

You should also include links to your products in the story ahead of time. Don't be afraid to make a soft pitch of your products early on. Most people will never read to the end to see the final plug. The purpose here it to move them towards the checkout.

Outsource

This is a lot to take in, I understand. It's complicated and time consuming. I never said that you had to do it all yourself though. There are options for you. Don't fret.

On some of the sites that we work with, we outsource the blogging or portions of it. Let me explain further. Using a site like Elance (they are changing their name to UpWork), I have been able to post writing jobs and find incredible writers. The cost of these bloggers can range anywhere from $10 a blog post to $100 a post and you often get what you pay for.
I prefer to post a job as 4 introductory blog posts. I ask them to bid on the cost of 4 blog posts to use as trial period. Ideally you are

looking for someone for the long term. You don't want people cycling in and out. It's just more complicated and tougher to teach them how you want the blogs completed.

I personally stay around the $15 price as it's what I'm willing to pay for each post. Remember this is just for the text. When you get it back it will still need work. You may also have extra costs if you want graphics or proofreading.

Try and get feel for the writer ahead of time. I always post what our website is about and what they will be writing about. I ask that they are comfortable with the writing topic and I also try and match the writer with the feel of the site. Don't underestimate the tone you are looking to convey. It's important.

If you are selling fishing gear, you probably want someone comfortable in this world. Do they know the lingo? Can they talk the talk? You want them to be able to relate with your readers and customers. If you don't want to publicize your url in the job posting, don't. Just make sure once you have narrowed down the herd, that you give them the url and the chance to review your site.

You want to make sure they are comfortable with you, as much as you are comfortable with them. Once I agree to have someone write for us, I make sure they are willing to sign an agreement formalizing the terms.

You need to make sure you are protected. You will be paying for ownership of the writing. You don't want anyone to be able to claim ownership at a later point. You also want to make clear there are no extra royalties that they receive later on.

Protect yourself up front so there are no surprises later. For a free copy of the agreement that I use, you can go to http://www.longlivetheinternet.com/blog-book. I can't make any claims to the suitability of the agreement for you. I always recommend you consult with an attorney to make sure it covers your specific case.

Once you have a signed agreement, Elance has a great escrow process. You can make each blog post a milestone. You don't have to release the funds for each post until after you receive it. I use PayPal to fund the escrow. The money sits with Elance until you agree to release it. This makes the blogger comfortable while protecting yourself.

After your agreement is signed and your escrow is funded, you want to discuss details. You want to make clear what you are looking for in your post.

I prefer to do the keyword research myself and then provide the blogger with it. I generally let them run with the Title, story and blog post. I give them the keyword phrase for each post.

I also provide them with explicit instructions. I outline the things that I want included in the body of the blog post. We will go over those later in the book. I just want to be clear with the blogger up front though. The better the instructions, the less editing you will have to do later.

Lastly it's important to understand that outsourcing doesn't work in all cases. For example on Long Live The Internet we don't outsource any of our blog posts. We are trying to connect with our readers.
I want you and any other reader to feel that connection with me. When I write and tell stories on the site I want people to know they are true and honest. But that is not an ecommerce site. My primary goal there, is to build a community.

On my ecommerce sites I'm trying to build sales. This is where the balance of "giving them what they want" and "building a community" comes into play. For the ecommerce blogs, I like it to feel approachable and casual but can be written by anyone.

This is a preference that you will have to decide for yourself. You have to decide the angle you want to take with your brand and the tone. If you are the face of your online store, then maybe outsourcing is not an option. Maybe you should be writing all the posts yourself.

Its your call but don't overlook outsourcing all or portions of your blogging process.

Hemingway

Whether I write the posts myself or not there is an incredible tool that I must share with you. I never much liked writing when I was younger. I viewed it as a necessary evil. As I get older though, I find myself enjoying writing.

In some ways, its helps provide clarity and direction. There is no better way to reflect on a problem or process then trying to write about it. As you put the words on paper, your brain begins to wander. You end up thinking of things you hadn't considered before.

I wrote an entertaining blog post about this if you are further interested.

For the purposes of staying on topic here, I will get straight to the tool that I use. There is a website called the Hemingway App. You can paste or copy your blog post into their online tool. Instantly the site reviews your writing and highlights troubled areas, sentences, or words. You can change your content in real time to make your post easier to read.

The Hemingway App works on an interesting principal. They explain it more eloquently, but I will try and break it down for you. The principal is that readability defines how well something is written. The more people can understand, the better somethings written.

Hemingway App makes your writing bold and clear.

The app highlights long, complex sentences and common errors; if you see a yellow sentence, shorten or split it. **If you see a red highlight, your sentence is so dense and complicated that your readers will get lost trying to follow its meandering, splitting logic — try editing this sentence to remove the red.**

You can **utilize** a shorter word in place of a purple one. Mouse over it for hints.

Adverbs are **helpfully** shown in blue. Get rid of them and pick verbs with force instead.

Phrases in green have **been marked** to show passive voice.

You can **format** your *text* with the toolbar.

Paste in something you're working on and edit away. Or, click the Write button to compose something new.|

They grade the readability with a number. The lower the number the better written the text is. The number corresponds to the education level needed to understand your writing. The lower the grade level, the more people can understand what you have written. A higher grade level means your writing is confusing.

If people are confused, then what's the point? Effectively communicating means that everyone should be able to understand. Hemingway wrote at a 5th grade level and the average American reads at a 10th grade level. You should try to have your writing score at a 4th grade level.

You have to try it to see for yourself. It's free and I can't recommend it enough. It cleans up a lot of my poorly written sentences.

P.S. This section of the book got a Grade 5

5

Dressing It Up

You're taught when you are little not to judge a book by its cover. You see people and instantly form opinions. It's wrong.

We know we shouldn't do it. Not only shouldn't we do it, we have been proven wrong many times. I've done it myself and feel terrible about it. Unfortunately, appearance means everything online.

About 10 years ago I was getting gas late at night. I ran inside to grab an ice tea. When I came out, there was a guy sitting on the curb outside the convenience store.

He looked disheveled and I thought he was homeless. As I came out of the convenience store, I handed him my change. He politely took the money and then looked at me with a face of disgust.

He said "I'm not homeless."

I shrunk to about 6 inches tall and apologized profusely. I quickly made my way back to my car and told my wife.

She thought this was hysterical.

Here I am trying to do a nice thing, and I completely insulted this guy. I made an assumption based on his appearance. I will never forget that day and my wife continues to make sure I don't either.

Unfortunately, appearance is everything. Regardless of experiences like this, we continue to make opinions and assumptions. We see things or people, and judge them based on how they look.

We can't stop ourselves. Its human nature. So if we can't beat them we have to join them. For this book we are going to focus specifically on the appearance of our blog posts.

This is actually a true story and excerpt from a blog post I wrote about appearance of your online store that you can read here.

I Like Some Blogs and Dislike Others

I read a lot of blogs. I'm constantly looking for other entrepreneurs and their stories. I have found the best way to learn is to listen. A wise man once said that you learn nothing by speaking. I'm not sure it's entirely true but I love it. Since blogging myself, I find myself reading a lot more blogs.

It's clear that some are great and others not so much. It's not necessarily that one person is such a great writer and others are not. Surprisingly some terrible writers actually had blogs that I liked. Others that were great writers had trouble keeping my attention. I started looking at these blogs further and dissecting them. I wanted to know what differentiated a good blog from a bad one.

Assuming that the topic is the same, and that the person can tell a good story, what was the difference. To my surprise it was the appearance. The last thing that I ever thought would make an impact.

Pictures are entertaining. Pictures break up the monotony of words. They help people visualize things, engage the reader, and improve the quality of your blog post.

One of the ways to easily differentiate your blog from others is to make it look good. The appearance of your blog is so important. Unfortunately you may have written the greatest blog post ever. If it doesn't look good, few people may ever read it.

People are lazy. We talked about this when we discussed Listicles as popular blog types. Listicles work because they are broken up in to little pieces. People can skim them quickly and get to the meat without reading the entire post.

I believe that every blog post, at the least, should have its own custom image at the top. What I'm referring to are title images. These are the images that draw your readers in. They give some color to what may not seem so exciting.

Below are two examples of blog images that are at the top of a blog on both our site and my wife's site.

6 ATTRIBUTES OF *successful* FASHION JEWELRY STORES

 Instantly, a custom graphic gives credibility to your blog. Most people don't know how, or don't take the time, to create an image for their blog posts. This is a mistake.

Besides credibility, graphics provide entertainment. They are fun to look at. They break up the text and often can help clarify difficult subjects. Pictures allow you to relate to your readers. Show a visual to keep the reader engaged.

If you are mentioning one of your products in your blog post, show it. Don't use the boring white background picture either. Use a picture where it's being used or worn or whatever it may be.

Use action shots to show people what the product looks like "in the wild." Go ahead and make that image linkable and link it back to your product page.

If you are telling a story, include an image to help them visualize. Like my story above about giving money to a man who wasn't homeless, I included a picture of me covering my face in shame. It's entertaining and keeps the reader interested.

If you are telling someone how to do something, show screenshots or photos of you doing it. If you are talking about celebrities or people who did something, try and find pictures. Images are worth a 1000 words. (Ok maybe not to Google but everyone else they are)

If you can't find photos or don't have them, make graphics. Taking a simple heading and making an image out of it can do the trick as well.

Graphic and Photo Sites

You now understand the importance of graphics and images. But, where do you get them? How do you find them or make them? A little while back, I wrote a blog post about 20 different sites you can use. These sites offer free images or are sites for creating graphics.

If you don't feel like diving into these details now you can skip to the next section on outsourcing your graphics.

1. Unsplash – The first of our free blog graphics site is a personal favorite. I have used Unsplash for a while now on many of my blog images. Their work is beautiful but often a little dark. Unfortunately the images are not tagged so they aren't search able either. You have to dig for ones you want.

2. Cupcake – This is a curated collection of images from photographer Jonas Nilsson Lee. He offers these specific pictures to be used in any way you please. A nice selection of high impact shots mostly of nature. Unfortunately they are not searchable either.

3. Flickr – The monster owned by Yahoo. Most people don't realize that Flickr has the ability to search for Creative Commons. These are images that can be used commercially for free. This site is probably the most powerful of all the sites I use. The bad is that you have to search through lots of poor quality photos to find the good ones. This site is a treasure trove of free blog graphics though.

4. Bucketlistly – Pete R who is the owner of the site actually created a cool site to let you track and share your bucket list travel plans. This particular part of the site is to share free high resolution travel photos. There are the standard mountain shots but lots of other expansive shots. They make for a great background to your free blog graphics.

5. MMT – This site is owned by Jeffery Betts who posts photos each week. Most of the imagery are New York related but there is a nice selection of "real" shots. Less staged and a nice feel.

6. Magdeleine – A nice selection of free photos to use for your blog graphics. The nice part about this site is they let you search the images. You can also browse by category or even color. Some great stuff to make free blog graphics here.

7. Design Shock – Our next site is actually one that offers free blog graphics. As opposed to just the background imagery they offer free sets of icons, and other items. You can use these in conjunction with images to make your blog graphics. They email a great free bundle every once in a while that I usually save for use later.

8. Gratisography – One of my personal favorites this site offers cool pictures. All pictures are photographs taken by Ryan McGuire. They have a cool edge to them. These aren't your traditional landscape photos. They are artsy.

9. Foodies Feed – If you are looking for food shots then this is a great option. They offer a nice selection of food related images that you can use for your blog. Often there are a couple angles of the same shot. This can be great to find one that works for the specific blog graphic you are working on.

10. Life of Pix – This site is a collection of photos submitted by others. You can use these images free of charge. I particularly like the curation here as the images seem a little more real. They are not as scenic and mostly great captures of moments.

11. ISO Republic – This is a great collection put together by Tom Eversley. Tom is a designer and photographer from England. He put the site together to offer designers a cheaper option. His images are categorized and there are some great shots here to use.

12. Super Famous – This is a collection of images from Dutch designer Folkert Gorter. He is based in LA now and the photos are predominantly scenery and nature. Nice powerful shots.

13. Morgue File – A large collection of images from various photographers. This site has a great variety. The ability to browse by category as well as color scheme is convenient also.

14. StockSnap.io – Stock Snap offers some great punchy imagery. As opposed to the somber landscape shots, they have a great variety of vibrant photos. They offer this site to drive people to their new graphic design tool. It's like the tools we are going to outline below to help you build your free blog graphics.

15. re:splashed – A collection of 400 images. You will notice some of the images from other sites but they have a nice mix of both nature and society shots.

Sites to Customize your Images

Now that you have all these amazing images and stock files, you need to do something with them. It's not enough to stick one of these beautiful pictures in your blog. It works to some extent but you really need to personalize it. Our final couple of sites are just for that. These sites will let you turn your images into amazing free blog graphics.

16. Canva – This site is my top recommendation for building your free blog graphics with no experience. Canva allows you to upload images from any of these sites above.
Once you upload the image, they have templated designed themes. You can add graphics on top of the images as well as text. The program is incredibly powerful.

I highly recommend you sign up for this free site and start playing around. If you are graphically inept or an advanced designer, this site is great. I use Canva to make my free blog graphics as well as Instagram posts and Facebook images. It's a winner.

17. Pic Monkey – The major competitor to Canva, Pic Monkey offers almost the same thing. My allegiance has been with Canva because I started using them first.
Pic Monkey's free version has banner ads on the page. You can upgrade to a paid plan that has no advertising. Pic Monkey is also a great tool to make free blog graphics. You can upload images and lay text over them.
You can make collages or all types of different graphics.
Surprisingly the main thing that I love about them is the ability to

crop an image. It sounds so simple but this is missing from Canva that I find annoying.

Another sweet option on Pic Monkey that Canva doesn't offer is the transparent background. You can make images that are transparent for use on your blog. Both huge features that Canva lacks. If you can get over the ads, it's a great option to make your free blog graphics.

18. Pixlr Editor – If you are looking for something a little bit more sophisticated then you should take a look at Pixlr Editor. This is closer to a full featured Photoshop type program. It's more complicated to use than the two prior options. If you are looking for something like Photoshop but don't want to spend the money, Pixlr Editor may be a great choice. It's a more advanced way to customize your free blog graphics.

19. Paint – The original basic image editor that comes with windows. This program is bad and leaves a lot to be desired. If in a pinch though you can change the images you got and add some text over them. This is probably the worst of the options. The only reason I can see using this is if you are stuck on a plane and don't have internet access. Otherwise use one of the three other free blog graphics programs I mentioned above. This is a last resort.

20. Adobe Photoshop – The granddaddy of all photo editing programs, Photoshop is serious. This is not a beginner's tool and has taken me years to figure out a fraction of the things it can do. It's incredibly powerful but expensive. Photoshop is not free although now Adobe offers a monthly subscription plan. Unless you have exhausted your other options, I can't recommend spending the money on Photoshop. The program though, allows you to do anything, if you can figure it out.

Graphic Outsourcing

What's that you said? You can't be bothered to make the graphics or images? Not so fast. It's really not an option. You absolutely must have some images or graphics for your blog to be effective.

Don't worry. I have a solution for you as well. Because I work on so many different sites at the same time, I can't possibly do all the images and graphics for my blog posts.

This is where you can use a freelancer again. We talked about using a freelancer from Elance or any number of others site for writing your blogs. Now we are going to look at finding a freelancer to handle your graphics.
Don't confuse the two roles. Someone who is a great writer is not the same person who is going to make your blog post look great.

My wife uses two completely different people to handle these tasks.

She has someone who writes each week. She then has another person who makes the graphics for the post. They are working two weeks apart from each other. The next post is always waiting for the graphic designer while the blogger is writing another post.

This is a great way to make your posts look professional for a marginal cost. You can expect to pay anywhere from $10 a post to $50 a post depending on what you want. I'm paying about $15 and they are cleaning up the HTML and formatting the text to look nice as well.

Make Sure You Are Covered

We talked about having your writer sign an agreement when freelancing. You also want to make sure you have an agreement signed for your graphics work. You want to make sure the graphics will be yours to own and keep after you pay for the work. You also want to make sure the designer doesn't use any images that are copyright protected.

You have to be extra careful with images and photos. Just because the graphic designer pulls it off the internet, doesn't mean you can use it. You may be liable for royalties or a licensing fee. Have the designer indemnify you and agree to only use copyright free or licensed images and graphics. The extra level of security up front can save you from a big headache down the road.

Spacing and Font

One of the simplest ways to make your blog post easier to read is white space. There are lots of fancy studies on white space but we won't get into them here.

White space: Also known as the negative space of a page or the portion that is blank or unmarked. It's a graphic design term. It can relate to blank portions in the margins, gutters, space between lines, columns, section, graphics, etc.

Increasing the size of the white space makes things easier to read. Let's look at the following two examples.

The big brown fox jumped over the little black log. He ran behind the big red barn at the corner of the yard. He patiently awaited the mouse to follow before pouncing on it.

The big brown fox jumped over the little black log. He ran behind the big red

barn at the corner of the yard.

He patiently awaited the mouse to follow before pouncing on it.

The only difference here is spacing. Clearly the second version is easier to read and easier to follow. Let's take this a step further.

Font is also one of the factors that can set the tone for your blog. While there are some nice fonts that are quite elaborate, you just want people to easily read your blog post. Less fancy fonts often work better for increasing readability. Make the font dark in color and contrast heavily with the background.

Increase your font sizes and increase your white space. You want to improve the readability and get out of the readers way. Below are two screen shots from two separate blogs which I won't mention. You tell me

rrom.

And the story of what they did to grow from a fledgling startup to a powerhouse with more than 150,000 customers is just as fascinating and valuable.

We talked to David about the lessons he's learned along the way about growth

I haven't manipulated these images at all. They are exactly how they appear on my screen. There isn't even a competition.

In summary, be generous with your white space. Use a larger font size and don't get too cute with your font type. Simple is better.

Subheaders

Another overlooked step to structure your blog is to break the text up with headers. If you load a page and see one big, lousy, chunk of text, what are you going to do?

You know the feeling. It's the same feeling you get when someone sends you a five million word email. You don't even want to read it. It's that feeling of exhaustion. You are bored before you have even started reading.

It's too much. You need to break up your text and give people bite size pieces. You should break up your blog post into sections whenever you can. These sections each will have a larger, bold heading. This helps give the reader some grounding and some sense of progress as they read.

It also gives readers the chance to skim the header sections. They can then decide if they want to read them. Make sure your header sections are enticing and informative. Stress the benefits of the section for the reader to make it more appealing.

Between headers, you still may get wordy. You still may end up having large paragraphs of text. Blogging is a little different than formal writing. Don't be afraid to break paragraphs up every two or three sentences.

You don't have to be formal about it. Give the text space and give people some white space. Let them easily get through the sections.

Lastly, we are going to use a trick that I learned from Brian Dean over at Backlinko. This site is primarily about search engine optimization.

Brian refers to little snippets that you insert in your text as Bucket Brigades. The term comes from passing a bucket from one person to the next along the line. What we are trying to do with Bucket Brigades in our blog post, is to keep people reading.

Whenever you see a chunk of text that seems long and boring, stick a bucket brigade in like so.

Bottom Line: People get bored and if they are bored, they head for the exit.

You see how that got your attention. You can stick them in anywhere that you think people are losing interest. Here are some great examples of other Bucket Brigades you can use to keep the reader with you.

- Here's the deal:
- Maybe you're wondering:
- But Why?:
- Now:
- What's the bottom line?
- You might be wondering:
- This is crazy:
- It gets better/worse:
- But here's the kicker:
- The Truth Is:
- Want to know the best part?

Bucket Brigades and headings are a great way to keep you reader interested and on your site.

Are you getting the idea here?

We are trying to ping pong the reader from a story to pictures and on to headers and bucket brigades. We are entertaining the reader like a court jester. The longer you keep them on your site, the more likely you are to convert them into a sale.

[6]

SEO

Oh SEO. Good old search engine optimization. As some would have you believe, SEO is black magic or smoke and mirrors. Let's take a look first at what search engine optimization is.

Search Engine Optimization: On-site and off-site factors to maximize the number of visitors to your website by having your website ranking higher in search engine results.

So let's dissect that further because I know there are a lot of skeptics out there. Let's first dispel the myth that there is no such thing as SEO.

Google has an algorithm they use to power their search engine. In simple terms, they have an equation they use to decide which sites are shown, when people search for something. This algorithm is extremely complicated and constructed of 200 or so different factors.

Google won't share the exact recipe to their algorithm because its their special sauce. This equation is why people search on Google. It's the core of why they are better than Bing or Ask.com or any of the other subpar searching options. Google doesn't want competitors to know their special sauce and they don't want people to game the system.

If everyone knew the secret recipe, then everyone would manipulate their sites to climb in the rankings.

Now let's look at the flip side.

Do you really need the exact recipe? We already know quite a lot. There are factors that we know work. There are things that we can do to improve our chances. While we don't have the exact recipe we have a good idea.

And with these factors, we can greatly improve the chances our site will rank higher in Googles search results.

> **Disclaimer:** This is not an exact science and things are changing daily. The following are tried and true techniques that I'm using today. Tomorrow is another day and things may change. You also may hear varying opinions of these

techniques. Like I said, only Google knows the real formula. We can just report what works for us.

Blog Titles

Let's start with one of the most important SEO factors for your blog. The title of your blog post is crucial. Your blog post title must have your specific keyword phrase in it. For example with our "Floating Keychain" example we wouldn't want our title to be "6 Keychains that Float."

While it may work based on other factors, we are trying to maximize our chances. We want to rank for the specific phrase "Floating Keychain." That's why our title should be "6 Floating Keychain Options You Didn't Know About" or some variation of this. Note that the exact keyword phrase is in the title.

Not only is the exact phrase in the title of the blog post but it's close to the front of the title. Google places an importance on the proximity of your keyword phrase to the beginning of the title.

For Example:

"6 Floating Keychain Options You Didn't Know About"

Is better than

"6 Brand New Options of Various Floating Keychains"

A simple change puts the keyword phrase up front and lets Google know it's important.

But What about Length?

Size matters. Your title should be at least 40 characters and not longer than 60 characters in length.

40 is long enough to provide you with enough words to rank for extra long tail keywords you hadn't thought of. Titles more than 60 characters won't be shown in the search results. You don't want your title cut off on Google search results.

Even worse you don't want Google selecting an alternative title because yours didn't fit. If you want to see how your title will look in search results, you can use the Moz.com Title Emulator.

The Slug

When you actually publish your post your url will be created. Your software will generally use your title to make that url. The url is the link to the actual post on your website. What's created is often referred to as the slug. Below is the slug as it appears in search results.

The slug is important for a couple reasons. People see this url in search results. Additionally Google uses it to classify and index your page. Your slug should include the exact keyword phrase that you are targeting. Ideally your slug is similar if not identical to your title.

If you are using WordPress or some of the other ecommerce platforms, you are able to customize this slug. It's often hidden but can be changed. If you are using a site like Shopify or some of the other ecommerce sites, you have to be careful here. They often create your blog url slug as soon as you publish your post. **Warning:** Make sure you title is properly spelled and finalized before you click publish. Some platforms won't let you change your url once the post is published and you will have to live with it as is.

Keywords in Your Copy

The actual body of your blog post is where Google gets most of its information. While they consider many other factors on and off the page, the text of your post is the meat. This is the part Google uses to decide what you are writing about and how relevant it is.

In the early days of the internet you could just stuff your blog post with your keyword phrase. Including the keywords over and over again increased the posts relevancy. Those times have changed and Google is far more sophisticated these days.

Google has built an incredibly powerful algorithm. Part of its strength, is the ability to relate similar words to one another. They are looking for variations of your keyword phrase. They consider alternatives of your keyword phrase.

When people write about a particular topic, it's only natural to refer to it in a couple of ways. Maybe in one sentence, you are writing about the plural of your keyword phrase. In another you are using different words entirely to refer to the same thing. The fancy terminology for this is latent semantic analysis or LSA.

While SEO with LSA is not an exact science, I will let you know what's currently working for us. You can decide what to use for yourself.

The most important keyword phrase is the one you selected to optimize for. It's the same keyword phrase that you use in your title and your slug.

This exact keyword phrase should probably appear in your post between .5% to 1% of the words. Depending on the number of words in your post this may vary. In a 500 word post maybe 3 to 4 times would be enough.

The next thing we are going to want to do is use related keyword phrases an equal number of times throughout the post.

Let's look at our example of "floating keychain." This is the keyword phrase that we were optimizing for. That means it will be in the title and the slug of the url. Additionally we want it in one of the section headers of the blog post and in a total of about .5% to 1% of the content.

For the second part, we want variations of our keyword phrase scattered throughout the content. For example we would want to include "keychains that float" and "floating key rings" and a couple of the other terms. These terms are from when you first searched for your keyword phrase.

You want to use the variations that were 2nd and 3rd place in search volume. This is what Google is expecting to see. Sprinkle a couple of these in the body of your post. Don't overdo it. If you have a 500 word post, then 5 or 6 total placements should be good. This includes both your exact keywords and your variations.

What we are doing here is making it clear what our post is about. We are focusing on our keyword phrase and surrounding it with other related keyword phrases. This is why it's so important to define your keyword phrase before you start writing your blog post. Coming back later to change your blog post can result in an awkward read.

Your Images

We talked about images in your blog post and how Google has a difficult time understanding them. The good news is that there are ways to assist them.

When you include images in your blog post, you want to do a couple of things to make sure that Google treats them accordingly.

1. You want to name your files with your keyword phrase or related keyword terms. For example maybe you took photos on your digital camera and uploaded them to your computer. They are probably named something like **DSC5162015.jpg**. This is useless.

In the folder that the images are stored you will want to rename your photos. Go ahead and name them useful names using a dash between the words in the filename. For example: **aqua-colored-floating-keychain.jpg.** Once done you will use these images in your post.

HINT: You should be doing this for every image on your online store. Not just on blog posts. On product pages and everywhere else.

2. The next step is to use the ALT tag. The ALT tag are the words that appear before the image is fully loaded on the screen. It also provides crucial information to Google about the image. Google uses these tags to understand the image. Go ahead and use keyword phrases in your ALT tags. For example: **Aqua Colored Floating Keychain**

Almost all ecommerce platforms allow you to change these ALT tags. Sometimes it's hidden away or not in the most obvious place. Take the time to hunt down where you change it for each image. Again you should be using the ALT tags for all images on your site. Not just your blog posts.

3. Use the image caption or description part to go one step further. This is the text that appears underneath images and is visible to people. Go ahead and describe the image further. For example: **This is the Acme Aqua Floating Keychain**

These three tricks are instrumental in explaining to Google what the images are about. This will help with the relevancy of your blog post and go one step further.

If you remember earlier in the book we looked at an example of a search result on Google. It was in the section about **Understanding Google Search Results**. Below is the image again.

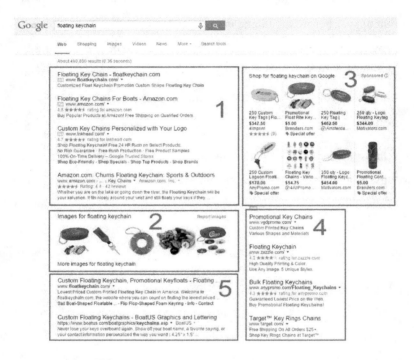

You will see that section 2 shows images from various people's sites. These image results are organic. Implementing the 3 tricks mentioned above can get your images showing in this section. This is one of the easiest places to rank in search results.

For some reason people don't optimize their images for search engines. Apply this throughout your site and you will be amazed at the number of search terms you can easily start ranking for.

Meta Description

When you perform a search on Google, underneath each entry you see a description of the page. This information can actually be defined by you. You can enter this summary so that it shows underneath the search results. Below is an example of what my wife has on one of her pages.

Ettika Boho Jewelry – Online Jewelry Boutique
www.loveandpieces.com/collections/ettika-boho-jewelry ▾
Ettika Jewelry is a mix of boho chic with laid back luxe. Found the world over Ettika Bohemian Jewelry was dreamed to life by Ettie Rafaeli and Joey Rafaeli.

In almost all ecommerce platforms you are able to type in your own meta description. You should include your keyword phrase in this description and make it sound appealing. You want to draw the reader in to click on your site. Don't be lazy and cut and paste a sentence from your blog post.

This is an extra way for you to show Google that your page is relevant and related to the keyword phrase. It's important though that you write your own description. Remember though that Google does what they want. They still may choose to use an alternate description on some search results. Often they will grab a sentence in your blog if they find it more appropriate to show the user. The description shown can vary based on the search terms you enter.

Links in your Blog Posts

One of the last items we are going to talk about to optimize your blog are links. Let's first start by defining links and backlinks.

Backlinks or Links: Inbound links from other website to yours, or in-site links to pages within your website.

Anchor Text: The actual words that are linked to the page on your own site or on another site.

If somebody links to your site with the words "bird catcher" that is a backlink and the words "bird catcher" are the anchor text. Those words and the link are indexed by Google. They use this data in their algorithm for website ranking.

We have talked about all the on-page elements to optimize your blog post. Linking though, is one of the most important factors. Let me simplify Googles search algorithm to explain.

The site with the most backlinks for the words "bird catcher" would be deemed the most relevant. This means they would show number one in the search results. So when someone searches in Google for "bird catcher" they see results. The results show sites sorted by the number of keyword matched backlinks.

As we discussed before there are hundreds and hundreds of other factors to ranking. This above example is oversimplified and flawed in some ways. It's exaggerated to make the point. Backlinks are one of the most important factors in ranking. These can be links from your site or from other people's sites.

In the next section we will talk about getting those links and the importance of them. For now we want to focus on your own links.

Internal Links

Google indexes your entire site along with the links that you have to other pages on your website. One of the best ways to help define what pages are about are to link to them. This means that in each blog post, you want to try and link to other blog posts you have written.

Furthermore you want to make sure that your anchor text is related to the post you are linking to.

Let's assume I was writing a post about bird catchers and I had an incredible bird catcher floating keychain. I may link the words "floating keychain" in my blog to the prior post that I optimized for floating keychain.

This helps build authority for that page. As Google crawls your site they will see that you have linked that page with the words floating keychain. They shows them that the page is clearly about floating keychain. I try and aim for at least two links to other pages within my site on every post.

You can link to products or collections or other blog posts. This helps build the credibility of other pages on your website or blog.

WARNING: We talked about not optimizing more than one blog post for the same keyword phrase. We want to go one step further. You never want to use anchor text matching keyword phrase and point to another page.

For example if we are optimizing a post for the term "Floating Keychain." Within that post we should not be using those words to link to another page. The goal here, is to make it clear, that this page is the best resource for that term. If we linked away from this page for those words, we would be sending conflicting signals.

Other pages should be linking to this page with the term "Floating Keychain." If you want to link to your actual floating keychains in your store then use another term. Make sure the links are something like "Click Here" or here is our "German Aqua Keychain from ACME."

Each page on your website should be optimized for a keyword phrase. Don't send mixed signals.

External Links

Another thing that Google likes to see in your blog posts are external links. These are links to other sites on the internet. Generally speaking, informational blog posts often link to other resources and sites. This is a natural occurrence and one that Google likes to see.

You should aim to link to at least one external site in each blog post. These links should be to credible sites that are related to the theme of your online store. For example, my wife interviews people on her blog once a month. One of the questions that she asks them about are their favorite jewelry designers.

She then links the designer names to their websites. Not the designer she is featuring but the designers they like. Remember we are optimizing the page for the designer she carries. We would never link to that designer's page. We want Google to feel that this page is the best resource for the designer.

She doesn't sell these other brands that the designers mention. They are often high authority, jewelry relevant sites. Google likes to see that you are linking to relevant sites and credible sites.

If you don't have an example like this, site a New York Times article or link to a Wikipedia definition.

HINT: Your ecommerce platform often has options when you are creating links. You can define whether the link will open a new window or keep the same window.

If you are linking externally, I always recommend you have it open a new window. This way it leaves your site open in the background. Hopefully when they are done investigating your external link they will come back to you.

7

Sharing Your Post

You have spent a lot of time finding the keyword for your blog post. You then wrote a wonderful post that is extremely entertaining and valuable. You then dressed up your blog and put in some great graphics. You then optimized the blog and got it ready for the prime time.

So now it's just a matter of publishing your post and watching all the traffic roll in.

Right?

Wrong.

You aren't done just yet. You actually have to spend a comparable amount of time promoting your post. Without backlink juice and credibility, your site is just sitting out there in cyberspace. Sure it's perfectly optimized and looks and reads great.

Let me give you an example. Let's assume your blog has an interview. Here is what I mean.

This is the equivalent of getting an interview. You then spend a couple of days researching the company. You take copious notes and you learn all about them. You rehearse what you are going to say and the answers you think you may have to give. You then fix up your resume and make it look perfect. You proof read it a number of times.

You go get a haircut and a new suit. Now it's the big day of the interview and you take a shower and get all dressed up. You brush your hair and your teeth, grab your resume and then sit on the couch. You don't move from there. You just sit there.

Are you going to get the job?

This is your blog at this point. Ready to perform and perfectly prepared. But you have to get to the interview to actually get the job. Getting your blog post in the hands of influencers and sites that send you the traffic is crucial.

Let's look at some different ways to do this and some tools you should be using.

Webmaster Tools and Analytics

Google offers two amazing free tools. Google Webmaster Tools and Google Analytics should be your best friends. Both of these you absolutely must be using if you have an online store. Let's look at them further and how they can help you get insight into your blog.

Webmaster Tools - The easiest way to get Google to pay attention to your site is to tell them you exist. One of the first things you should do if you haven't already, is setup your webmaster tools account. This tool, from its name, is designed for webmasters. Don't feel intimidated. It's not so fancy.

The first step in setting up your account is confirming the ownership of your website. Depending on your comfort with technology there are some different ways you can do this. Some of them are as easy as logging into your GoDaddy account if you purchased your domain name there. Others are a little more detailed. They have step by step instructions for you to follow. One you claim ownership of the site, Webmaster Tools will take a couple days to populate with the pertinent information. Webmaster Tools provides insight into how Google views your website. They will show you what's working and what's not.

You will also be able to see any errors with your site as well as other websites that are linking to you. Webmaster Tools will alert you to any broken links or other content or pages that are not showing properly. It will show you best practices to ensure you are displaying your content the best that you can.

What we are going to focus on is indexing your site. Indexing refers to including your pages in their search. The easiest way to do this is to submit your sitemap to them. Your sitemap is a list of all the pages on your website. It includes your blog pages and all your product pages.

Almost all modern ecommerce solutions now update the sitemap automatically. When you publish new blog posts or pages on your site your sitemap is updated. Once Google knows the location of this file, it will automatically come back to read it. The more they come back and find new content, the more frequently they will return.

To submit your sitemap you will navigate to the crawl section and find the part titled sitemaps. Once here you will click on "Add Sitemap" and will submit your sitemap. Depending on the online store you are using, the locations may differ.

If I don't have your site on the list below, feel free to contact us through the site at http://longlivetheinternet.com and Bob or I will be more than happy to assist you.

- Shopify Users: www.yourwebsite.com/sitemap.xml

- Volusion Users: www.yourwebsite.com/google_sitemap.asp

- BigCommerce

Users: www.yourwebsite.com/xmlsitemap.php

- Magento Users: (mostly)

www.yourwebsite.com/sitemap/sitemap.xml

- Wix Users: www.yourwebsite.com/sitemap.xml

- Yahoo Small Business: www.yourwebsite.com/sitemap.xml

Once you have submitted your sitemap, Google will confirm that it was received. They will validate the link and you are all set. This location doesn't change and this is how Google will know when you have updated your content. It visits this page and checks to see if there is new content. When it finds new content, it adds it to its search index.

Google Analytics - The next tool that you need to have installed on your site is Google Analytics. This is another free piece of software from Google.

Analytics is a little piece of code that you will add to your website so that Google can track all visitors. This information is absolutely crucial to an online store. You are able to see countless data points, but let me list some to give you an idea.

- What search terms people are searching for when getting to your site

· What links on other sites are bringing traffic into your store?

· How long are users staying on each page of your site

· How frequently are people leaving or bouncing after landing on your site

· What's the average duration of peoples stay?

· What is your ecommerce conversion rate (number of sales/number of visitors?)

· What page are people exiting from your site?

· How many clicks are coming from your advertising channels?

This is just a short list of the data that you can collect from Google Analytics. This is an important part of your blogging campaign.

This tool will let you see exactly which blogs are driving traffic. Which blogs are converting to sales? Which blogs are people bouncing from quickly? Which blogs are ranking higher in the search results? This data can help you become a better blogger and also focus on what's working.

If you are getting a ton of traffic to one blog but nobody is clicking through to your product than you can make changes. Revisit the post and add some links to your products. Clean up the message and drive them where you want them to go.

You will setup an analytics account in the same fashion as your webmaster tools account. You will need to add a bit of code to the site. It's not complicated.

A simple Google search of "How to add analytics code to my <your ecommerce platform> site" will do the trick. Just make sure to replace <your ecommerce platform> with Shopify or Volusion or whatever you are using.

Time for Business

Now that we have the tools in place to monitor the traffic and your sites, it's time to get down to business. It's time to share and create traffic to your blog.

Backlinks

As we mentioned before, backlinks are the foundation of your sites authority. Google ranks this factor alone probably higher than any other.

Because of this, you need to be looking for ways to build backlinks to your blog posts. In our other book "How To Start an Online

Store," I discuss some simple backlinks. You should make sure your friends, vendors, and partners have links to your website. This is the easiest way to get your initial backlinks.

Once you start blogging though, you are going to want to build backlinks to each of your posts. These backlinks build the credibility of the specific post and help raise that page in the search results. But how do you get those backlinks. How can you earn them?

Over the next couple of sections we will look at various outreach approaches. These approaches help get your blog post shared and linked to.

Email Your People

We have talked about the importance of building an email list. I really focus on this in our other book. We talk about how you can do this and when to start.

In this case, every blog post should have an opt-in at various portions of the blog. Email has proven time and again to be the most effective way of driving traffic. This traffic then ultimately converts to sales on your site.

Blogging give you a perfect way to reach out to people by email. What better excuse do you have then to email someone about a new blog post on your site?

There are only so many times you can email someone about sales or specific product offerings. Your blog gives you a chance to mix it up. This gives you a chance to talk about something different.

If you are providing relevant interesting content, then people will be interested. If you don't want to spend the time to make a fancy email, just use the same graphic from your blog post. Write a couple sentences teasing the subject of the blog and end it with a "Read More" link in the email.

This helps drive traffic to the blog and hopefully into your store. Ask your email followers to comment on the blog. Ask them to share it on their social sites.

If you don't ask you won't get. These are your core people and are most interested in what you have to say. Ask them to help and you will be surprised how many do.

Get Social

If you aren't already active on Facebook, Instagram, or Twitter, now is the time. Part of building a following and repeat business to your store is building a face to your store. I don't necessarily mean a person.

I'm talking about a brand voice. You need to show what your brand offers. What do you stand for and let people feel comfortable they are buying from a real company.

When you do this, you will slowly build a following on social networks. These people are your army of spokespeople. Whether they just "Like" your stuff or actually share it, they can increase your footprint. This footprint is where you will be making sales. This is your audience and reach. Ask your people to share your new blog post. This helps expand that reach.

Join related Facebook groups and share your new post there. Ask these people to share the post if they find it helpful. When you publish a new blog post, you should be sharing it on all your social networks. Get people to answer a question and engage them. Draw people in to get them interested in the post.

On your blog, you should have share buttons that are prominently displayed. This lets people share your post on the network of their choice. If the buttons aren't present, people don't think to share them.

Do you have an amazing quote from your blog post you want people to share? Try placing a little button from a company called Click To Tweet on your site.

This cool feature lets you create a simple button with your quote and link already loaded in it. You embed this into your blog post and when someone clicks the button, it automatically opens twitter to share. Inside the share window has your quote ready to be tweeted along with a link to your site. This greatly increases the rate of shares on Twitter that you post will get.

At the very least, you should be sharing on all your social networks. The more the better. Here are some of the most common ones that you should consider using if you don't already. It can take 2 minutes to share on each.

- Google+ both your personal page and the business page
- Facebook both your personal page and the business page
- Twitter
- Instagram
- LinkedIn
- Tumblr
- Flickr
- Pinterest (pin your pictures to a board about your blog)
- Reddit
- Scoop.it
- Quora

Reach out to Influencers

One of the most overlooked and most powerful methods to have your blog shared is to promote it. Decide which sites you have seen the most success from.

Certain industries lean towards twitter and LinkedIn while others only use Facebook, Pinterest, and Instagram.

You know your market and you know your industry. Once you have published your post, you want to go to these specific networks. From here you will look for specific influencers. Generally you want people with upwards of 500 followers. When you are just starting out, you can't focus on the biggest influencers. Remember they are approached by everyone.

Look for people that have similar styles to your store. Make sure their followers align with your demographic. The next thing you want to do is look at the information they generally share. Would your blog post be interesting to their followers? Would it be beneficial to you if it's shared?

If you think there is an alignment, then reach out to them. It important to complement them and then tell them why you think your blog would be interesting to their followers. Ask for them to share if they find it interesting.

You should be emailing people, tweeting people, direct messaging them and reaching out to them in any way that you can. Don't be discouraged, this takes time.

Most people won't share but the ones that do can be powerful. This may even result in one of their followers re-sharing it. Keep a list of people who share and remember to reach out to them on future posts.

You must promote your content to reach new audiences. This is the way to build your audience, build your backlinks, and ultimately build your sales online.

Commenting on Blogs

Over the years, this particular technique has been given a bad rap. I still think this next method is a powerful one. This slower approach helps build awareness for your site and your blog posts. Most blogs have a part at the bottom for you to comment or leave a response to the post you just read.

This is a great place to make a contribution to the blog and other readers. Additionally you are softly promoting yourself.

Many of these comment boxes let you include a link to your site. Some will ask you for your name, email, website, and comment. When you fill this out, your comment often goes to moderation.

What this means is that the owner of the blog must approve the post before they agree to let it go live. Go ahead and give some kind words about the post and point something interesting out. The point here is to further the discussion.

If you can actually provide some further value to the post you are far more likely to have your comments published.

This does two things. If you are providing value to the conversation people will look to see more about you. Your name is often linked to your site and results in traffic. Besides the traffic, Google will index the backlink to your site. This adds to your credibility in the search results.

Try and comment on blogs related to your site. Your goal here is to attract people that will buy from you.

Besides commenting on blogs, you can answer questions on various question sites. Sites like Quora and Yahoo Answers and Reddit are great places to answer questions. You can show your knowledge and build your credibility. In your response, you can often include links to your individual blog posts. Answer the question and link back to your blog post that may be related.

This helps build your backlinks and reputation. Before you dive into Reddit you may be interested in reading Bobs post on 7 Tips for Getting Started With Reddit. You see how I just weaved that link into the content there? That's exactly how you would do it in your comments.

RSS feeds

The last thing we are going to talk about is having your blog syndicated on various sites. You may have heard the term RSS before. This is what we are talking about.

RSS: Rich Site Summary is a format that feeds each of your blog posts to other sites on the internet.

Just about all ecommerce platforms with a blog, have a built in RSS feed. This is the feed for your specific blog. This feed looks like code when you view it in a browser.

Depending on the ecommerce software you are using, you can google to find out the location of your RSS feed. Once you have the location you are going to want to submit this to different RSS feed sites.

These sites will syndicate the content on their own site as well as others. Most of these RSS sites offer plugins for other sites. People place these plugins on their sites to show relevant content. When you publish new blog posts they may be featured in these plugins on people's sites. This is more exposure for your blogs to drive traffic back to your site.

Below is a list of some RSS and directory sites that you can submit to. Some of them are paid and others are not. Not all these sites are created equally so take a look and decide whether it works for your category and brand.

- Alltop
- DMOZ
- Best of The Web
- Blog Catalog
- Spillbean
- Feedage
- Blogdigger
- IceRocket
- FeedShark
- FeedCat

8

It's Your Turn

I commend you for seeing this through. You have made it to the end but it's your beginning. Don't worry. I'm not leaving you high and dry. As I have mentioned throughout this book, we have a blog where we want you to join us. It's absolutely free and we cover topics related to all types of online business.

We walk you through blogging techniques that are working for us. We also look at many other case studies. We are constantly testing things for our online sites and we show you what works and what doesn't. We cover marketing and more technically oriented topics.

So what I'm saying is come join us. Bob and I welcome you to the family. Post a comment on a blog and please make sure to join our email list. We send out updates and have a free gift for you.

I have put together an amazing resource guide with over 50 resources that Bob and I have used to make over $1,000,000 online. Additionally I have links to all the sites we mention in this book. Lastly I have the agreements for freelancers that I mentioned.

To get this free gift you can go

to http://www.longlivetheinternet.com/blogging-book